W9-CON-873

RED, WHITE, AND BOOM!

Lee Wardlaw

illustrated by Huy Voun Lee

HENRY HOLT AND COMPANY
NEW YORK

Red, white, blue
Curbside view

Flags unfurl
Batons twirl

Bugles call
Marchers tall

Glossy boots
Gloved salutes

Whistle drill
Fifers trill

Shoulder seat
Thumping beat
July 4th drums down the street!

Blue, red, white
Tugging kite

Frisbee zips
Doggie flips

Spike the ball
Picnic sprawl

Corncob sweet
Drippy treat

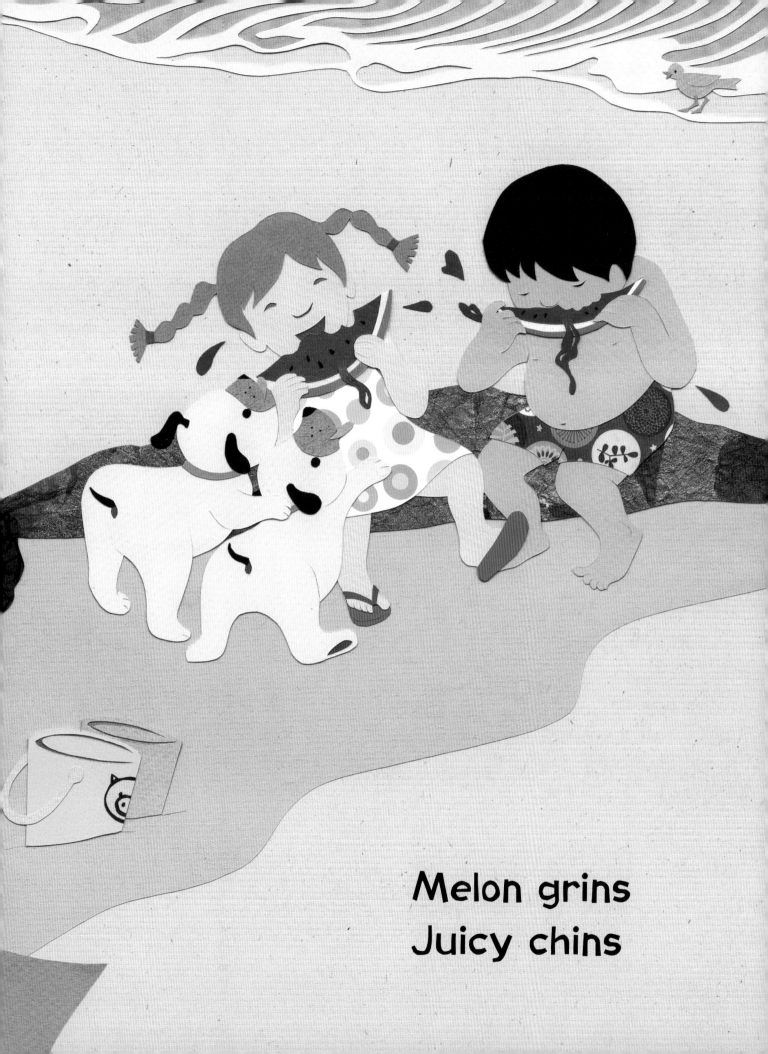

Melon grins
Juicy chins

Hot-foot dash
Splutter, splash

Castle moats
Seaweed boats

Shoulder seat
Seagull fleet
July 4th with sandy feet!

Fireflies flit
Sparklers spit

Pinwheels spin
Goosebump skin

Peacock plume
Sunburst bloom

Star flakes spill
Heart-thump thrill

Rockets wing
Crackle, sing
Burst and zoom
Red, white, boom!

Ooohs and ahhhs
Cheers, applause

Shoulder sighs
Drowsy eyes

White, blue, red
Sleepyhead
July 4th parades home to bed.

For the staff at
Santa Barbara Montessori School
with love and gratitude for all you do
to celebrate the child
—L. W.

For all Americans who make
America beautiful and unique
—H. V. L.

Henry Holt and Company, LLC, *Publishers since 1866*
175 Fifth Avenue, New York, New York 10010
mackids.com

Library of Congress Cataloging-in-Publication Data
Wardlaw, Lee.
Red, white, and boom! / Lee Wardlaw ; illustrated by Huy Voun Lee. — 1st ed.
p. cm.
Summary: Parades, beach picnics, and fireworks in the park are
some of the ways Americans celebrate the Fourth of July.
ISBN 978-0-8050-9065-9 (hc)
[1. Stories in rhyme. 2. Fourth of July—Fiction.] I. Lee, Huy Voun, ill. II. Title.
PZ8.3.W216Re 2012 [E]—dc23 2011018541

First Edition—2012 / Designed by April Ward
The artist used cut-paper collage to create the illustrations for this book.

Printed in China by Macmillan Production Asia Ltd., Kwun Tong, Kowloon, Hong Kong (Supplier Code: 10)
1 3 5 7 9 10 8 6 4 2